SHARDS OF GLASS

SHARDS

OF

GLASS

A Kaleidoscopic Life's Memoir

FRANCINE GLASSER

Epigraph Books
Rhinebeck, New York

Shards of Glass: A Kaleidoscopic Life's Memoir
© 2021 by Francine Glasser

ISBN 978-1-954744-32-5

Library of Congress Control Number 2021914278

Book design by Colin Rolfe

Epigraph Books
22 East Market Street, Suite 304
Rhinebeck, NY 12572
845.876.4861
epigraphps.com

kaleidoscope *noun*

1. : an instrument containing loose bits of colored material (such as glass or plastic) between two flat plates and two plane mirrors so placed that changes of position of the bits of material are reflected in an endless variety of patterns
2. something resembling a kaleidoscope, such as:
    a. a variegated changing pattern or scene
       // a kaleidoscope of colors
    b. a succession of changing phases or actions
       // a kaleidoscope of changing fashion
3. a diverse collection.

—Merriam Webster.com

shylock *noun*

Loan shark, usurer, moneylender, pawnbroker, money-monger, lender, broker, gombeen man, payday lender and extortionate moneylender.

—wordhippo.com

INTRODUCTION

IN THE LATE summer of 2020, my husband and I decided to brave the Covid pandemic and drive an hour-and-a-half away to upstate New York for a brief getaway. Heading out from our home by the Hudson River, it felt freeing to be in the Catskill mountains. We drove into the beginnings of the kitschy part of the Catskills and came upon a sign stating: THE WORLD'S LARGEST KALEIDOSCOPE. Without so much as asking my spouse, I took a sharp turn into the parking lot leading to the exhibit. I had a strong compulsion to witness this kaleidoscope phenomenon.

I have loved kaleidoscopes since I was a child, when I especially loved the magical way objects shifted and changed shapes with the turn of my wrist and a blink of an eye. Nothing remained the same, but it all fell into place, creating amazing beauty with each new formation.

We paid our admission fees and were told to lie down on a carpet and look up at a large screen overhead. Music was blaring from a surround-sound speaker system, pulsing with bass notes that accompanied the rhythms of the light show above.

Lying under the spectacle above us on an uncomfortable rug, enveloped in the noisy music, I began to fade away and had some strange, tingling bodily sensations. I didn't know what was happening but did know that it led me to memories, times, and places I had left behind that I hadn't wanted to return to—especially lying on my back under the World's Largest Kaleidoscope. I was feeling exposed and vulnerable, so I told my husband that we needed to leave right away. We left abruptly, and the clerk at the ticket booth shot us a snarky look.

It was nothing personal, yet it was *very* personal. From this strange kaleidoscope experience erupted a story I realized I had to tell. The barricades I had carefully erected suddenly shattered like the shards of glass in the giant kaleidoscope, and I was finally free to share with others the story of my childhood. Was it the best childhood—no, but it certainly wasn't the worst. It simply left me as an adult with as many challenges as gifts to cherish. I'm not seeking pity, maybe just validation and empathy. Actually, all that I seek to do is to finally tell my story and be done with the remnants that still linger.

Δ Δ Δ

I AM THE daughter of a man with a gambling addiction, and my family was constantly on the run because of Dad's problem. Whenever we settled into a new town it would only be a matter of time before we had to leave in the middle of the night. Sometimes we were being chased by shylocks or loan sharks—and at other times by landlords or ex-bosses. Sometimes it was just the best moment to leave so dad could follow an employment lead or a dream. By the age of eight, I had already lived in a wide variety of states and communities and had attended seven or eight different schools.

We stayed in many different houses, apartments, motels, family homes—and even at a babysitter's house—when between apartments and due to many other experiences, I often felt fragmented, and over time my identity seemed broken into sharp shards. But this also gave me the gift of a spectacularly kaleidoscopic view of life on the run and of the people we'd met along the way.

I was a frightened, precocious little girl who became defiant by default and saw the world as unsafe and unpredictable. I also was blessed to see the earth as beautiful and exciting, creating a kaleidoscopic world view. I was always, always, always waiting for the other shoe to drop. And it always did, with a resounding thud. The emotional and psychological foundation of my childhood was built not on solid bedrock but on a sinking sludge of quicksand.

My dad has been deceased for almost twenty years now, and it's time for me to tell my story and to imagine what my life could have been like if we had stayed in any of the homes we landed in—if we hadn't had to let go of our belongings and dreams, again and again—if we could have sustained friendships with other children, with teachers, with people in each town and community we came to. How life might have developed if only we could have stopped running from the madness. This question continues to haunt me. As I write these words, I am lying on my mother's couch in a house we purchased for her after my stepdad died, right down the road from where Dad is now buried. There's something synchronistic about this that brought my parents home miles apart from one another. Another gift that I was given was a box of childhood slides and film my dad had taken that had survived all of our moves. These were treasures that told the story of my youth and, in a visual way, confirmed and challenged some of my memories.

After we'd stopped moving from place to place during one of Mom's and Dad's separations, Dad changed his name to an alias and lived on and off for many years in a Hasidic Hebrew community in Brooklyn, New York. He prayed and davened alongside the ultra-orthodox Chassidic men and was given room and board in exchange for odd jobs he did in the community. Once, days away from my first marriage, Dad tried to marry me off to a man in his community. I recall having become angry with him over this, for I saw this as personally insulting and violating my boundaries.

Throughout those years I was ambivalent about Dad living with this religious community, yet I felt compelled to visit him, but I was scared that once I got there I'd be inadvertently absorbed into the community and wouldn't be able to leave. Paradoxically, I now belong to a Neo-Chassid Renewal Jewish Congregation, a hipper form of my dad's earlier affiliation.

The people in the Brooklyn community never knew that my dad was hiding within their tightly knit ranks and that not far away he had another identity as a husband and father. When my dad died, members of the Hasidim came to show respects at the burial. There was an unusual storytelling by their rabbi, honoring my father as well as his alias. Everyone left the service feeling satisfied that their loved one was honored. The rabbi was brilliant in how he wove kaleidoscopic meanings around my father's life experiences. He told a story of King David (David was Dad's alias) along with Dad's real name, Irving (God Wrestler). Rabbi wove together metaphors and biblical stories, creating an integration through which to tell the story of Dad's life struggles. Dad didn't have to run from the shylocks any longer and was finally laid to rest, freed from wrestling with God.

Growing up, I was very protective toward my younger sister and tried to shield her from our parents' constant arguments about money. While I always made sure that she was safe, I was also terribly dependent upon her. She was born during our trek to find stability out West, and she is five years younger than me. She was my best friend as she got older, when friends were a fleeting commodity, and I needed a friend who I didn't have to leave over and over again.

I came to understand my father's addiction to gambling when I discovered that I, too, had many compulsive and addictive traits myself. I finally had to forgive my father for making us live like refugees. Before Dad died, he apologized for causing all that chaos in our lives, but he still reminisced about gambling at the racetrack until he died. At around the age of sixteen, I realized that I had inherited compulsive and addictive behaviors. I took to shoplifting clothing and jewelry from neighborhood department stores and friends' houses. I also began compulsive eating at this time. Because there was so much deprivation in our lives, I found unhealthy ways to get my needs met. I was also sexually compulsive in the 1970s.

These days, I particularly love having a full refrigerator because back then it was nearly empty much of the time. We shopped using food stamps and had to suffer the stigma attached to this. I recall people whispering and pointing at us on the grocery store line as we checked out. I eventually became a compulsive overeater, consuming tons of sugary items and junk food. Later on, I entered recovery to relearn how to nourish my body with a healthy, balanced diet. I love nothing more than having a fully-stocked refrigerator, as that makes me feel blessed with abundance and security.

The last item of clothing I purchased before becoming a compulsive spender and debtor was a black, front-snapped jumpsuit. I was sixteen years old at that time. I bought it on layaway and would stop into the boutique often up until I paid for it in full—purchased with my earnings from part time employment. I felt a sense of pride and privilege in being able to buy a unique outfit from an upscale boutique. In my forties, I entered recovery for addictive spending. My spending seems to be a compulsion to regain all that I lost and was left behind during my childhood. Today, I gravitate toward thrift and second-hand stores and find it a great challenge to purchase new items of clothing. I seem to be driven to acquiring other people's discarded treasures—over and over again trying to gather all that was left behind. I love to pick up used items from curbside giveaways and clothing swap-gatherings. New items have no appeal for me. I must say that I have enough money to purchase new things from stores, but I just can't seem to do so without guilt and shame.

After focusing on how I was affected by Dad's compulsive behaviors, my resentments have faded, and I have a new focus on how these life changes have made me the multi-dimensional woman I have become. I am whole, yet I have shattered pieces of glass inside, and I am a living kaleidoscope that can change in a moment and become beautiful and brilliant with the turn of a wrist, but it also can have dark colors within that create dark thoughts and musings.

I am the proud survivor of a challenging, sometimes heart-wrenching, life, yet I bear witness to the turns of the wheel that transformed a disrupted life into one of wholeness, stability, and hope.

Moving seven or eight times and attending two kindergartens and five elementary schools before the age of eight gives a glimpse into my childhood. My developing vocabulary included the word *shylock* from a very young age, which I understood to mean the bad men who frequently caused us to uproot our lives and leave everything behind. I often felt like I had been living the life of a foster child—but I didn't change parents, just homes. Sometimes it seemed as though we were a homeless family having to keep searching for shelter. Since I used to run a foster care agency as a social worker, I know that refugees and military families and ministers' children and nomads have experienced much more pain, loss, abuse, and neglect than I ever have, but I still had many things in common with these "people on the move." I've heard that there's a syndrome called *ghosts' kingdom*, where— when children of different races are adopted by opposite-race families, these children often make up fantasies about their true parents. Clarissa Pinkola Estés has a story of "The Mistaken Zygote," where a stork dropped a child into the wrong family's chimney, so the child always felt like an outsider in that family but didn't know why. The child's real family could have been right around the corner, but, oops, what an accident.

Defiance became my middle name, and while living in a house in St. Louis, I defiantly laughed when scolded by my father as he hit me with his belt for being fresh. Then he hit himself and said, "Ouch, that hurt," as I ran to my room before he could catch me and hit me again. I was a know-it-all who truly knew nothing.

Much of my story is based on factual memories, and some of it is recalled from a more psychological stance, as I'd sometimes create an imaginary reality to shield me from our life on the road through escape by fantasy.

What I'd like to share is that I lived in many places due to my father's gambling addiction, so we were often on the run. Each time we settled into a new town it would be only a matter of time before we would take off and leave in the middle of the night to go to our next destination. The continual moving also affected my mother and sister and any pets we might have had at that time. Although we would leave our belongings behind, probably ending up tossed onto the curb awaiting the garbage pickup, my mother says that she had always rehomed our pets. When I asked her recently what actually happened to our beloved dog TIFS, she said she didn't remember and that he must have died, because we wouldn't have left him behind.

Denial ran deep in our family consciousness. The losses for a little girl were profoundly sad and difficult to process. Our lives were like the shapeshifting of images and twists and turns of the kaleidoscope. Yet the kaleidoscope needed to be held to the light, and since we had much darkness and the darkness often shattered our hopes, dreams, and stability—sometimes the light just couldn't get in.

I found a way to manage the pain and disappointment by imagining splitting off from my family and staying behind to experience a rooted, rather than uprooted, life. True, this was a temporary and imaginary solution, and eventually I'd awaken from my fantasy to return to the reality of life on the run. Separating myself saved me from losing my sanity, and along the way I collected many survival treasures to fill my spiritual kaleidoscope. Fantasy allowed me to envision life as I wanted it to be, not as it was.

Moving to new places to live can be an unsettling experience. The way a home feels and smells is essential to my welfare and more important than its curbside appeal or price tag. Having lived in so many different residences, the feel of a place always held either a certain pull or an aversion for me, and it still does. If a place didn't feel right, I would leave it as soon as possible or find a safer place to go to for a while in my imagination. I was often told that I had a great imagination if only what I imagined were true. If a new place felt right, I could more easily settle into and adjust to it. It was in nature, and especially in the woods, that I felt the most at home. To this day I head to camp at a nearby campground with my tent and dog and lay awake at night listening to the owls calling to one another to come home. Nature is like a psychological and spiritual compass directing me to safety and wholeness. Trees and stones and wildlife were safe, and I had much to learn from nature. The forest accepted me. I was never an outsider. Safety became my primary objective because I was a scared little girl, powerless over all of the changes and transitions in her life, who was soon to become a brave yet still scared adult.

My sister is five years younger than me and has no recollection of our instability, or of our housing insecurity. It rubbed off on her—but differently, as she doesn't recall the chronic goodbyes and doesn't recall the traumatic episodes. It's as if they never happened, and it's as if we had experienced two different childhoods. Both my sister and my mother have accused me of making up my deeply held memories. At times this feels like being gaslighted, and I respond with anger and sadness, feeling quite alone with my remembrances.

Growing up, our refrigerator was often as barren as driving down Route 66 in the middle of the night, which definitely contributed to my compulsive eating. I have received help for both of my compulsions, and I have had to forgive my father for making us live like nomads due to his addiction to gambling. I used to deeply resent both of my parents, but now I cherish memories of Dad and have developed a strong relationship with Mom. Today, I wish to focus on ways in which these life changes made me whole and beautiful—like a shattered piece of glass in a kaleidoscope rearranging itself into a beautiful image.

I bring the wheel of my understanding of a disrupted life into a life of wholeness and stability. I recall always having to be the new girl in a new school—and a shapeshifter, fitting chameleon-like into the new setting, trying to make new friends quickly before it was time to leave yet once again. We would leave with or without warning, and mostly without time to say goodbyes and gather friends' addresses for sending cards to keep in touch. I often didn't get to attend birthday parties I'd been invited to due to having to move again.

If social media had been available in 1965, my life would have been less fragmented, and I would have been much more able to maintain relationships over distances.

THE JOURNEY BEGINS

My KALEIDOSCOPIC JOURNEY exemplifies how my life was, how I managed, how I was shaped for my future—and how we always had to pick up and pack up and leave. Being a child, the choices were either to become invisible or to cooperate with my parents' decisions. Some of my memories might be distorted. I try to recount events as remembered, and then my fantasy life often takes over when the stressors are heightened.

Every move left memories and cherished belongings behind—as well as beloved pets and toys, friends and connections. I will take the opportunity to tell of the many inner children that were left behind to weave themselves into their new realities.

So the journey led us from Bronxville, New York, to: Flushing Queens, New York; Mount Vernon, New York; Tulsa and Catoosa, Oklahoma; and Kirkwood and St. Louis, Missouri. Then back to Queens and winding through Ossining, New York; Glastonbury, Connecticut; and finally, Mount Vernon, New York, for the second time. Sometimes we would move several times within one location. Whenever we landed at a new home we always had to move yet again. We returned to Queens for a while to stabilize—then Ossining, where my parents briefly reunited after having been separated for a while—then Mount Vernon, where my folks finally legalized their divorce before we eventually settled into our final childhood home. I couldn't feel grounded until my parents divorced, because we could never establish stability in any location as long as we lived with Dad's gambling.

Mom moved us from a Mount Vernon apartment to a more affordable rental down the road a bit, and then into our final home in a high-rise building also in Mount Vernon. Here, we felt like we had arrived home, since we were no longer running. The building reminded me of grandma's home with the cooking smells in the hallways. It had an elevator, the first one I had ever ridden on. I remember it being an adventure, and that the building had a grand lobby where I used to twirl around, singing and dancing when the neighbors were not watching.

This was the first time I was happy to be moving into a new home.

I had many thoughts and questions as we were heading down the highway toward Mount Vernon and fatigue had overcome us all, but we were also filled with hope and anticipation of where our future home would be, and what it would look, feel, and smell like. Homes come along with certain smells and certain energies; at least that's been my experience from living in so many different places. Will our neighbors be friendly? How are the schools in our new town, and will the kids accept me as the new girl at school once again introduced in the front of the classroom by the teacher?

My clothes were never like the clothing of my peers, as we were poor much of the time unless Dad won at gambling. Then we would buy all sorts of things that we had gone without for so long—since the last winning. During times of abundance, we were all well-dressed in stylish clothing, then we would have to move and would often leave our clothing and belongings behind, as we were crammed into a Dodge Rambler. We would purchase new clothing in our new town. If we were without money, clothing would be scarce and unattractive. To this day I have a compulsion for clothing and prefer to shop at second-hand stores even though I have enough money for new store-bought clothing. I always feel an affinity for used clothes that have been discarded, and I also feel that in some karmic way I am retrieving pieces of my past. These shards are essential facets of the kaleidoscopic travels my family endured.

NEW YORK

I was born in New York City, and my first residence as an infant was in Bronxville, New York, at Darling Avenue. I don't have any memories of my first home, and I couldn't have known that due to Dad's gambling I would be deprived of housing security and stability from age three to eight and a half years old, which would influence all my future choices, behaviors, and personal relationships.

Next, we moved in with my grandparents in Queens, New York. I was only about four years old at the time, and my sister hadn't been conceived yet. That's another story further on down the road that blends our family into an even fuller kaleidoscope. Dad had again gambled all of the money we had, and we lost our housing, leading us to move in with my grandparents temporarily.

My grandpa was angry and ashamed of my father; my mother tried to hide her worry and shame, and my grandma made us warmly welcome, remarking upon Dad's bad luck while preparing a warm meal for us.

Cherished and nurtured.
Scent of food in the hallways.
Family glued us together.

FLUSHING, QUEENS, NEW YORK

WE LIVED IN Queens for a few months, initially staying with my grandparents and then acquiring an apartment nearby. Dad was going to try to find work in New York City, and I loved my grandparents. We stayed in Queens for a while, but Dad couldn't find work so we prepared to take a life-changing road-trip adventure that my dad had been plotting and planning. There was always the mention of heading west, similar to the gold rush. He kept his plans in a personal notebook he had with him all of the time; it was a brown leather-bound book with lined paper. Nobody was allowed to hold his book or look in it.

I loved living in Queens with my grandparents and other relatives nearby—aunts, uncles, and cousins. The neighborhood was filled with Hebrew delicatessens as well as Israeli falafel cafes—and pizza too. All of the restaurants carried bottles of Coca Cola, which could be traded in for pennies at the candy store where my friends and I would then trade in the money for penny candies.

Dad was one of five siblings born to Jewish immigrant

parents. His father survived great trauma, having witnessed atrocities toward his mother while growing up in Russia during the pogroms. He made it to America scarred by the images of abuse he had witnessed, and this made him into a man consumed with rage and anger. He was a harsh disciplinarian and very critical toward my dad, often comparing him to my uncle, Dad's younger brother, who was an athlete and a scholar who grew up and studied medicine and became a highly acclaimed doctor. My dad looked up to his brother, and his brother looked after my dad. I just realized that their relationship was a lot like my sister's and my relationship.

My dad had struggled with his studies and might have had Attention Deficit Disorder. He always lived in the shadow of his brother's brilliance. Dad was a diamond in the rough, and his brother was the tumbled gemstone in their father's eyes. I didn't know much about my grandmother's upbringing, but she was joyful, good natured, caring, and loving to us all. She would always wear a housedress with a floral apron and orthopedic slip-on sandals. She and my grandpa would leave their dentures to soak overnight in these pink-colored plastic containers. The first time I peeked inside I was frightened by what I saw, as the teeth were looking up at me. Later, Grandma explained that the teeth needed to be removed to be cleaned then put back into their mouths. She would play card games with us, and she would always buy me rabbit's-foot toys to care for and to soothe my feelings, and I believed them to have magical qualities. I would go to sleep at night rubbing the fur of the rabbit's foot. She always had goodies for us to snack on, and I looked forward to this. I remember one night when I was going to sleep, but got sick, she came to comfort me and in the night's light. I could see that

7

underneath her nightie she wasn't wearing panties, and I remember thinking for the first time that she was a woman—not just a grandma.

My grandparents had a difficult marriage, as my grandpa would become aggressive at times. Dad's other siblings were a brother who got shot down in World War II and suffered with kidney failure for many years until his death, although he was the longest living dialysis patient in New Jersey, where he had lived. Dad also had two sisters who were verbally abused and possibly physically abused by my grandpa and suffered a great deal emotionally.

In Grandma's and Grandpa's marriage, whereas she was the caretaker, he was critical toward her and verbally abusive. At one point, Grandma went and lived with her son and daughter-in-law (my aunt and uncle) due to escalating physical and verbal abuse—only to return a year later and live her remaining time together with my grandpa. Grandpa was heartbroken when she left, and when she returned he never treated her abusively again, since he was so grateful to have her back.

My dad was very close to his mother and siblings and spent his life making amends for the devastation he caused with his gambling. He would often borrow and even steal money from family and strangers alike, never making restitution. He told me stories of how he had held up a bodega in the Bronx with a fake gun and demanded money from the cashier, walking away with five hundred dollars.

I was groomed as Dad's confidant at a young age. I loved my dad but held onto anger for years until I forgave him because he was so ill with a gambling addiction and some other challenges. He also might have had bipolar disorder, because he experienced the highs and lows of his gambling addiction. I too was afflicted similarly. Dad's addiction was the driving force to go West to find sustainable employment and get far away from the loan sharks that were in hot pursuit.

While still in Queens, Dad did find us an apartment, and it wasn't far from my grandparents' apartment. It was more modern, clean, and smelled of freshly painted walls. I remember while living there coming upon his playboy magazines tossed underneath the bed and looking at the pictures with confused excitement.

Mom was happy in this apartment, and we were content in thinking that this would be our forever home. But eventually Dad told us to pack up and get ready to leave, as he was moving us to a town about two hours away called Mount Vernon, New York, where he had found employment as a shoe salesman. He really wanted to get to Oklahoma but took yet another detour. Mom cried when Dad broke the news, and she tried to make me feel better, but she was too sad to pull off the facade. I didn't want to say goodbye to my friends at school and in my apartment building, and I didn't want to leave my grandparents and aunts and cousins and uncles.

My grandma was an angel and a kind-hearted healer weaving together the wounds that began to surface. Our grandparents tearfully said their goodbyes and gave us some money and food for the trip. I was afraid to leave the safety and stability of my family but had no choice but to go along for the journey. Some journeys can become fun, and I was sure that some of the trip would be a fun time. I was quite young, but I still have memories of that relocation.

Hope doesn't last.
Dreams make me free.
Missing the unknown.

ST. PAUL'S CHURCH, MT. VERNON, N. Y.

MOUNT VERNON, NEW YORK

WE ARRIVED AT our new apartment with a few belongings. We always had pots and pans and plates and silverware and drinking glasses. We lived in this apartment for several years.

My mother was slim and beautiful, and having been born in Paris and raised in England, she had a charming accent as well. Mom had already lost too much. During the Holocaust she had been a hidden child whose parents and sister had perished in Auschwitz. She was raised in an orphanage for five years until her eldest brother came to adopt her after learning that he had a sister who had survived the Nazis. She was raised by her brother and sister-in-law following the war.

Going to live with her brother was a difficult transition, and at first, she didn't want to leave the orphanage—just as I never wanted to leave our home in search of a new home. She didn't know her brother, who was twenty years older than she was, and did not trust going with this strange man. She also only spoke French at that time and had to learn to speak English as her brother and his wife, my aunt and uncle, resided in England. They became a family, and my mom graduated from high school and met and married Dad when she turned nineteen.

She met Dad at a Jewish dance hall, as he was in England on leave from the US Air Force during the Korean War. He was tall, dark-haired, and handsome with dreamy eyes and a good smile, and my mother fell madly in love with him. She had found someone to love and love her back—someone who could fill the void left by all the heartbreaking losses she had endured. Mother followed him back to the States with big dreams of a life of wealth, family, security, and love. She had lost everything stable in her life from the time when, at three years old, the Nazis took her parents by cattle car to Auschwitz. She survived only because she was ill at the time and in a nearby hospital. A neighbor heard that her parents had perished, so claimed guardianship of my mom from the hospital and hid her amongst her family. After all she had been through, Mom craved a life of stability and did not know that Dad was a gambler with a following of debt collectors tracking him down.

My mother had me when she was only twenty-one years old. She told me that when she gave birth to me, she felt terribly lonely because she had no family or friends in the States. She also told me that in the hospital expectant fathers were made to stay in the waiting room, pacing and handing out cigars. Childbirth was very different back in the sixties.

While living in the apartment in Mount Vernon I was told that we had had a beagle when I was a toddler, and I'm certain that he howled and barked a lot, as beagles tend to do. Mom was immediately faced with my dad's debts upon her arrival in the States, and she soon learned that all the promises that baited her into marrying him and coming to America were actually half-truths, and that he was a compulsive gambler and con man. But he was also kind-hearted, loved us, loved nature, and was an avid birder and photographer. He had served our country during the Korean War, enlisted in the US Air Force.

Our apartment was conveniently located about fifteen minutes away from the Yonkers Raceway, a trotting-horse track where my father would frequently gamble. As I grew older, he would often take me to the racetrack, and I would watch the enthusiasm of the gamblers—then the dejection, especially when Dad lost all of his money. All the losers would toss their bets onto the ground, and the scattered tickets seemed to form a kaleidoscopic display. It made me dizzy to look at it.

Sometimes Dad would win some money, but mainly, he lost his earnings and left us with very little to make ends meet. I would try to cheer him up to no avail when he lost all of our money. I would try to make him laugh or hold my hand, but he would become despondent and forlorn. It made me sad to see him this way, as minutes before, when he was cheering for his horse to win, he was elated. He would become agitated and irritable, almost like a different person, and sometimes this would scare me.

I grew up learning the lessons of trying to cheer up and care for those in pain. I've done this with lovers, friends, and with clients I have worked with. I found that these lessons worked with my clients but never worked with loved ones. I also learned that my heart would break often when caretaking failed to make my loved ones get better. I just learned to watch them crash and burn. I crashed and burned as well, as I loved intensely and lost painfully.

I would start to get that sick feeling in my gut, knowing that my parents would be arguing about the lost money all night long. Although Dad did work as a salesman and was a hard worker, he was always dreaming of becoming a millionaire someday. He chased that elusive dream, causing the ruination of our family. His gambling became much like the colors and designs of a kaleidoscope that can't be captured and are always out of reach and always changing and shining greater brilliance to lust after.

After Dad had gambled away our savings and stability, he tried to convince my mother that we needed to move to Connecticut to be closer to my uncle, Dad's brother. This time I imagined that we stayed behind and didn't follow Dad on his wild goose chase. I wanted to stay in my room with all of my stuffed animals and our beagle. I liked the smells of the good food Mom made and the nice clean clothes she dressed me in. I enjoyed our walks around town and around the local stores. The store keepers would pinch my cheeks and say how cute I was. I was happy.

All of a sudden, our daily walks stopped abruptly and Mom had to give our beagle away to some neighbors down the hallway from us. I remember being so sad at the thought of giving away my puppy, who was also my best pal. So we refused to leave in my fantasy world I created and in spite of Mom and Dad having lots of boxes in the living room and frenzied packing and discarding going on. Then Dad said that tomorrow morning we would be moving to Glastonbury, Connecticut. I didn't know what that meant, but I did know that I didn't want to leave my home and live someplace else. I was six years old at the time and fully understood what this meant. I was a precocious child, and I believe that was because I was acutely aware of our household and its challenges.

So we let Dad leave to find us a place to stay and we stayed behind in my imagination. I learned to be able to create a life of fantasy and imagination not having to face the reality of constantly changing homes, schools and pets. I think that it made Mom happy that we didn't have to move, although she didn't believe the imaginative worlds that I would create, and she cried a lot that she missed Dad. I missed him too, but staying behind was better than having to leave. We lived apart for a few years and heard from Dad occasionally, and he kept pleading with us to come back and live with him. He had found a new job, and as I was turning six years old now, he said that it was time to be together as a family again.

Mom had gotten a part time job as a keypunch operator, and we had enough money for the rent and for food to eat. There was no more fighting about money and Dad's gambling habit. Life was more peaceful, and I didn't get that tingling feeling in my belly that I had when my folks argued. Mom had started to date while separated from my dad, and her friends were nice to me, but I knew that she still missed being with Dad.

I went to a babysitter whose name was Vera when Mom was at work. Vera would give me milk with coffee and sugar, and would toast Italian bread under the broiler and put a slab of butter on it. We had this every day when I went there. We would watch television, and Vera's husband said that I reminded him of Gina Lollobrigida. I would miss Vera and Joe very much if we were to move as Dad wanted.

15

I started to wonder about where we were to live. I was afraid because I sensed the looming stress surrounding moving. For a few weeks after packing for Connecticut, Dad lost the apartment we were planning on moving into. I was heartbroken and didn't want to leave, so I created fantasies of staying behind in my imagination. I did my magic dance and I stomped my right foot and clenched my fist around the magical rabbit's foot my grandma had given me during the time we lived with her. I decided to create my own story of being left behind. And like a kaleidoscope splits off and creates new designs, and during the imagined separation of my parents, Mom and I traveled to England on the Queen Elizabeth II ocean liner for her niece's wedding celebration.

I remember getting seasick and having to take a blue-colored pill, the exact color of robins' eggs in a nest. This was due to the choppy ocean tides that cause motion sickness. Mom also got ill, and this part of the trip wasn't fun at all. Being on an ocean liner was a big adventure for a girl alone with her mother. I remember that we saw sharks circling the ship, which was kind of scary. I didn't know how to swim and I had heard about the Titanic ship sinking after hitting an iceberg, and many women and children dying, and passengers on the ship singing a song while the Titanic sank—which was sad when I thought of them all losing their lives.

While on the ship, the captain was very friendly and invited Mom and me to observe the engine of the enormous ship. The pistons smelled like metal and oil and grease and steam in the large engine room. It was a bit scary to be so little and to witness such power and noise and commotion. I was glad when our invitation was over. I played with the other kids on the ship and we'd sometimes eat our meals together. It took seven days to go from New York City to England, and seven days to return.

Mom's family joyfully met us at the seaport in England. Dad did see us off at the New York seaport, and we stayed at the fancy Waldorf Astoria Hotel in New York City the night before leaving. I remember jumping on the fancy bed, and when I was told not to, I said what's the difference and got in trouble for being fresh. Dad was sad when we left, and as it was, we stayed for several months because Mom wanted to spend time with her family. I do remember having had a great time once we got there, and everyone fussed over me, for I was still just a little girl. I got to dress up real fancy for the wedding and carried a flower basket as the flower girl. But while I was using the toilet, I placed my flower basket aside, and someone walked away with it. I was so disappointed that I broke down and cried. All of the ladies tried to comfort me, but I kept crying for my pretty basket.

Mom told me that she had dressed me in an adorable outfit of red and white and we took a ride on a double decker bus. As I was chatting away with the other passengers, Mom said that I was precocious and would talk to everybody. We spent time staying at my aunt and uncle's home and had a great visit. I remember trying lox for the first time and joining the grownups for high tea and crumpets and jam. But I missed Dad because, according to my passport, we remained abroad for over six months before returning.

PHOTOS

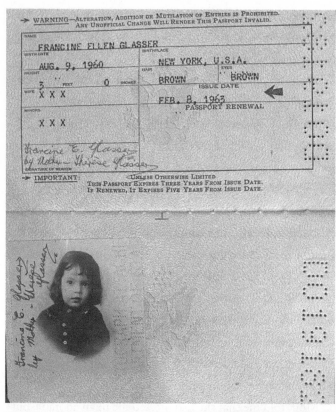

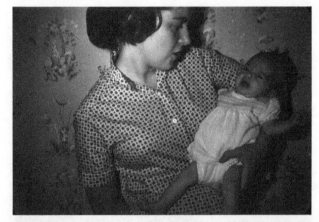

After our adventures to England, dad picked us up from the seaport and prior to heading west, as he had business to complete, we ended up being homeless for a few months and moved in with a babysitter, Catherine, whom my mother befriended. The home was warm, spacious, and lovingly furnished, but she served army-rationed instant eggs for breakfast, which I found disgusting. Catherine ran a daycare center for working parents, as in 1965 it was a new phenomenon for women to be in the workforce.

One night, I was to sleep in the same bed with Catherine's twenty-year-old daughter.

I became uncomfortable, getting that icky feeling in my belly, and I did not want to stay in the bed with Catherine's daughter, so I didn't. She said that she was going to kiss me. I stomped my foot and clenched my fist around the magical rabbit foot charm my grandma had given me earlier and ran down to my parents' bedroom off the kitchen.

As I stood outside their bedroom door, I heard Mom crying, saying *no* repeatedly as Dad yelled and pleaded that she turn over her diamond engagement ring so he could pawn it for money so they could find a place to live. While all of this was going on, I shivered in the kitchen without solace and comfort. Mom ultimately gave in and tearfully relinquished her beloved ring.

A year later, she saved up her money and retrieved the ring from the pawn shop. To this day, I don't know why she wanted it back after her marriage had ended so painfully.

Dad got the money for the ring, and we were prepared to leave in the morning, heading on yet another treasure hunt for our forever home. We said our thank-yous and goodbyes, and I didn't have to sleep in Mary's bed ever again, and that felt like a relief. Mom believed me when I told her about what scared me, so I slept in Mom and Dad's bed until we left.

While Mom and I were overseas, Dad moved all of our belongings from our Mount Vernon apartment out West to Oklahoma. He did this without telling Mom, and when he came to the seaport in New York City to pick us up, he surprised us with this news. I was now old enough to wish to return to live as a family, and truthfully, the separation never took place, and I released my imaginal fantasies to the universe, as I no longer needed them to save me. I only imagined it to be so as I didn't wish to move. Maybe I had a foreboding sense that there were many moves in our future. Dad had driven from Oklahoma to pick us up and move us there to be with him. This was shocking for me and for Mom—and where were my beagle and my dollies and toys? I started crying, as did Mom, and we got onto the highway and off to our new home.

The first leg of the journey proved to be a fun time, but after eleven or twelve hours in the car, we were all becoming hungry and restless. We had long finished the tuna fish sandwiches and soda pop my grandma packed for our adventure. I kept asking, "Are we there yet?" To which my parents answered in unison, "We will be there soon." We stopped at cheap motels along the way so Dad could rest up for the long drive ahead. We were driving to unknown destinations and unknown circumstances, hoping that life would be better than it had been up until now. This was the 1960s, and Mom didn't yet drive, so although Dad had to do all of the driving, he seemed to enjoy it. I would raid the candy and soda machines at the motels and would get great pleasure from stealing the soap and shampoo samples.

We stopped many times along the way to Oklahoma and made the best of the journey. We'd play car games, counting red cars and blue cars and other-colored cars. We would look at the license plates and keep track of how many people from different states we saw driving on Route 66 and on backroads at times.

Dad always looked into his rear and side view mirrors to make certain that we were not being followed by loan sharks and shylocks. This always made me anxious, and he would say that if anyone ever were to ask me where my dad was, that I needed to lie and not tell the truth and say I didn't know where he was. This was to protect our well-being. This kind of talk would make me nervous, because I didn't want strangers following and threatening us.

All in all, the road trips weren't too bad, as I didn't have to attend school at these times and feel like an interloper once again. Being on the road gave me time to rest and have time with my parents, and it created beautiful sights and sounds that brought me back to the kaleidoscopic visions of my disjointed life. I'd sometimes recall various friends I had made and having to leave them behind. These were the not-so-good memories, but I did know that there are always more friends to be made, and that nothing difficult lasts forever, and life and living are always changing.

Sometimes along the trip a carnival would be advertised when we stopped at a diner for a meal. I'd ask if we could go to the carnival, and Mom and Dad mostly said yes. I would eat cotton candy and go on the kiddie rides and have lots of fun, and Mom and Dad would be holding hands, which they rarely did nowadays.

Dad had been living in our new apartment, and I wondered as to what kind of apartment it was and what it smelled like. I imagined it had a woodsy smell, which we would enjoy. I wondered if there were kids to play with and if we could get a puppy so I could have a best pal again.

Toothless dollies.
Sage and drum beats.
Baby born into chaos.

TULSA, OKLAHOMA

WE ARRIVED IN Tulsa, which is the second largest city in Oklahoma and among the most populated cities in America.

Everything looked like it was covered in dust and was quite dirty looking. There were no high-rise buildings like we had back in Flushing, Queens. We arrived in the middle of the night, so we slept in the car that night and awoke to the sounds around us. We all needed to go to the toilet, so Dad drove to a gas station, and we all took turns. By this time, Mom's pregnancy began to show, and we openly spoke of her being pregnant, although I didn't comprehend what that really meant. We let her use the toilet before we did. We grabbed some snacks from the convenience store at the gas station and drove on to our newest residence. This was in a two-story apartment complex in Tulsa, Oklahoma. It was rundown and looked impoverished. There were broken-down cars in the parking lot.

We entered our apartment, as Dad had already obtained the keys, and the place smelled like urine. I didn't like the way it smelled or felt. There was very little room in the apartment and not much privacy for us. Mom said that she would use fabric to make separate rooms and create privacy. I'm guessing that this was all that we could afford on borrowed money. There seemed to be a broken playground with lots of kids just milling around in groups. This might be a difficult neighborhood for a new kid on the block. The kids all seemed to know one another and I couldn't find my way into their cliques.

I would visit our neighbors down the hall, the Choctaw family, and they would make me Native specialties like fried bread with either beans or, as a treat, powdered sugar. They'd also give me soda pop. I liked visiting them, as their children had been taken away. I didn't know what that meant, but anyhow, they treated me kindly, and I loved receiving their attention. We would play cards just like Grandma and I used to play—gin rummy, mostly. My parents liked when I visited our neighbors because they said that I talked too much and asked too many questions and they needed a break.

My aunt and uncle were living out in Talihina, Oklahoma, at that time and would come and visit us at our apartment on weekends. Talihina is in Le Flore County, and its name (meaning "iron road") came from two Choctaw words, *Tully* and *Henna*. Talihina was a bit of a drive to Tulsa. When our family visited, I felt embarrassment about our apartment, as it was cramped and had a weird smell.

When the family arrived, we would all gather into our respective cars and drive to a nearby park, eat a tasty lunch together, and look for birds and wildlife. For the time that they were there, time would stand still and there was no leaving and no staying—just these magical moments spent together. Sometimes we would all drive to a nearby Native American powwow. I looked forward to these outings and enjoyed the sights, sounds, smells, and tastes of the powwow. We sometimes would be greeted with the apprehension that we were Caucasian outsiders, but we mostly were welcomed. I wanted to dress and dance to the ceremonial smoke and drumming. If we stayed in Oklahoma, I would have liked to spend my time at powwows. As our visits ended, we would hug and kiss goodbye until our next get-together.

My aunt was attending a community college outside of Talihina and had an African American friend/roommate. In those days, no one would rent to a "colored person." Dad did a noble thing and went door-to-door until he convinced a landlord to rent to my aunt and her friend Gayle. We were all proud of Dad for doing this brave deed. This was during the 1960's, and the Civil Rights Movement was happening.

Dad and Aunt Irene would take my mom driving, even though she was almost due to give birth, and taught her to drive—and she got her driver's license. Sometimes we would all load up in the car and go to visit my aunt, uncle, and cousins at the Choctaw Nation Health Services. We were all so glad to be together again, and we built good memories. My cousins and I would hang out, play games, and eat good food, since my uncle could afford good, abundant food.

My aunt told me they joked that they would always know when Dad was visiting, as they'd hear Joan Baez blaring from his transistor radio as he approached their apartment. I too, liked to hear Joan Baez sing, as she has a beautiful voice that brings people to tears. Many years later, when Dad was in a nursing home ailing from Parkinson's dementia, I'd put his headphones to his cassette player on him and play Joan Baez, and tears would flow from his eyes down his cheeks.

My sister was born while we lived in Tulsa, and I was glad to have a little baby sister, but it meant that I had to share the living room in our already cramped apartment. Everyone was on edge with a crying baby in a tiny one-bedroom apartment. We lived like this for about six months, and then my parents bought a starter house in Catoosa, Oklahoma, with Dad's GI Bill subsidy and paid $69,000 for it! We were so excited, as this meant to me that we wouldn't have to move ever again.

We gathered our belongings and jumped into the car, looking forward to seeing our new home. The house was in Catoosa, Oklahoma. Catoosa was located near Highway 66, about fourteen miles from Tulsa. In 1970, the population was 970 people. President Richard Nixon designated the port of Catoosa as the northern end of the McClellan-Kerr Arkansas River Navigation System, which added needed commerce to the area.

Later, we got a white terrier pup named TIFS, after Mom, Dad, my sister, and me (Terry, Irving, Francine, and Sharon). This time, TIFS came to live in our new house with us, and this time we didn't have to give our dog away.

Our house welcomed us.
Cul-de-sac of friends.
Red velvet and gold,

CATOOSA, OKLAHOMA

WE ARRIVED AT our new home as the moving truck was carrying our furniture into the house. I prayed to my God that this would become our forever home. It was a great house for our family, located on a cul-de-sac where I looked forward to learning to ride my bike. There were lots of kids playing outdoors, and I hoped that they would welcome me into their games. One odd thing was that they had never met nor known of a Jewish person before, but they were kind, and that's all that mattered.

Our furniture was all set up, and our home was lovely. My dad bought me a princess bed with a headboard of red velvet and golden trim. My sister's bedroom had a crib and a toddler bed with lots of decorations in a childlike theme of giraffes and bunnies. My parents' bedroom was the master bedroom decorated in shades of teal, orange and red—and was beautiful and vibrant. We had a nice, bright, sunny kitchen, painted in oranges and yellows, and our living room had velvet furniture in a green color. We had a television set for watching our nightly shows. This home was my dream come true.

I attended second grade and was welcomed by the staff and by the other students, and I planted roots by making friends. My sister was always glad when I returned from school and would greet me gleefully with "Ya-Ya, Ya-Ya," as that's what she called me.

On Friday nights we would light Shabbos candles and say our prayers of thanks for all that we had and for our Sabbath meal. The fighting between my parents over money subsided, so maybe Dad had stopped the gambling.

I imagined growing up in this home and graduating from a local high school, and maybe marrying a local boy and raising a family together. I would make sure that he wasn't a gambler, and I would stay at home and care for our children. We could visit our family back East but would return here to our home following visits. I would care for my aging parents who might still live nearby.

THIS IS ALL I EVER WANTED! THIS IS ALL THAT EVER MATTERED!

About a year into living in this haven, the arguing began again, and I heard words like loan sharks and gambling. This didn't bode well for remaining in this home. Dad had gambled and had had to borrow money from loan sharks. They would come after us like a school of sharks looking to chomp on us and frighten us into paying back Dad's debts. The other shoe had dropped again, and we were forcefully told to gather what we could take in the car, and that we were heading for St. Louis, Missouri. We were crushed but did as Dad told us. I grabbed my dollies and a few items of clothes and a nightgown. I also grabbed a tiara I'd been given by my parents because I loved the Miss America pageants and wanted to be

Miss America someday. I remember crying when we'd watch the pageant and I wouldn't be chosen. Mom packed up my sister's belongings and her own, and Dad tended to his own belongings.

I decided that I wanted to stay here forever but couldn't come up with a plan to make that happen, as I was only about six or seven years old. Maybe I could ask my Sunday School teacher at Synagogue to let me come home with her, as she was kind and seemed as though she'd lived in the same home for quite some time. Or maybe I could go and live with my family in Talihina, but they were involved in my cousin's lives, and my aunt's schooling and my uncle's internship as a medical doctor. I searched my brain for someone I could trust enough to ask to live with because I didn't want to leave our beloved home and leave all of my memories and toys behind.

Again, we had to leave our puppy with neighbors who agreed to take her from us. This was a major move because we were leaving behind a home that we owned. I'd miss riding my bike with the other kids around our cul-de-sac and would miss the trick-or-treating on Halloween and dressing up in costumes and eating a variety of candy. I'd miss doing arts and crafts at school and learning to read, which I enjoyed most. I'd miss attending Choctaw powwow ceremonies and watching the dancers in their brightly colored outfits dancing to the beat of the big drum in the center of the dancers. I loved eating the fried bread sprinkled with confectioner's sugar. There was so much to miss, as I had really created roots in this home that I truly believed to be our forever home. But alas, it was time to let go and move on, as there was nowhere else to go. One last thought was to lie and tell my teachers that my parents were hitting me and be removed from their care and placed into foster care—but from what I heard, that wasn't always a better option. So I surrendered and got into the car, and we headed to St. Louis, Missouri. AND WE WERE OFF, again.

Vanities left behind.
Pets left behind.
Jet plane leaves Dad behind.

KIRKWOOD/ST. LOUIS, MISSOURI

We entered our apartment in St. Louis, and the space smelled old and musty. It was very dark and gloomy, and it made me feel lonely. I had my own room, which made me glad, as I usually had to share my room with my sister. It was a good enough place to live in and had lots of woods out back. I imagined a family of wolves living back there and wondered if they'd mind me meandering into their den and hibernating with them. I imagined this to the point that it became real in my mind, and every time I needed solace I'd turn to the family of wolves. Although I had a bed, I felt more at home sleeping with a sleeping bag on the floor. I felt nearer the earth this way. I'd have dreams that always involved leaving and arriving and being faced with anxiety about going to school on my again-first-day of a new school. Sometimes I'd cry out from a bad dream, but my parents would be loudly talking about finances and wouldn't come to me. I would have nightly dreams of being raised by wolves, and these dreams and images brought me comfort. I could imagine their coarse, dense fur and hot breath as I snuggled and tucked myself into them.

After a few months of living there, Dad and Mom planned a vacation for all of us. We never vacationed, we just moved, but this time we packed our suitcases on the day of our trip. My sister, Mom, and I sat with our suitcases awaiting Dad's arrival home from work, but HE DIDNT RETURN HOME FOR TWO WEEKS. He had gambled away the money for our trip and was filled with guilt and shame. We unpacked our disappointment and put away our suitcases. We sobbed when we realized that Dad had let us down once again.

There was a playground outside where my parents would let me bring my little sister with me to play in the daytime. She was a chubby little girl, and I was lanky and skinny. We got to the slide, and I could climb through the handrails and jump down. My sister was too little to do the same, but she copied me, getting stuck in the handrails, and got a large scratch that was bleeding down her belly. We went back to our apartment quickly and Dad yelled at me, blaming me for purposefully hurting my sister. I pleaded that it was an accident and kept apologizing. I never took her to the playground again. I truthfully thought I was too young to be supervising my sister, so I felt a sense of relief too.

I attended school and made friends as soon as I could. I was hungry for friends. I spent more time socializing than on my schoolwork. I was the only Jewish student in my elementary school, and during the Christmas chorale assembly the principal drew attention to me and thanked me for participating in the Christian songs, since it wasn't my religion. I remember that when the name of Jesus was sung, I would mouth the name but not sing it, as I had been taught not to say his name. I did attend a Jewish after-school class, where I made friends with other Jewish kids. I remember having fun there and eating cupcakes with the Star of David drawn on the icing.

At home, Mom was busily working on my Hanukkah gift. My mom worked endlessly on creating a coveted vanity for me for a Hanukkah present. There was lace trim and a mirror and a chair. It was coming out so pretty, and I loved that my mom was taking so much time and care in making it for me. I was so looking forward to sitting on the chair and having Mom brush my hair as I looked in the mirror. I imagined the mirror reflecting and refracting light as a kaleidoscope does. I couldn't wait for Hanukkah, as this was the only present I wanted. The night of Hanukkah arrived, and we lit our first-night Hanukkah candles. Dad didn't come home that night, as he had gambled our holiday and food money away. He came home a few days later after sleeping in his car.

He told us some story that he had run out of gas and pulled up to a hospital, which turned out to be an asylum, as he was cold in his car. He told the nurse there that he was feeling hopeless and suicidal, and they admitted him to a floor with pygmies screeching throughout the night. He said that he felt scared and didn't sleep for three nights. He then passed the evaluation that released him, as they had to keep him for seventy-two hours according to the state's mental health laws. I'll never know if this was the truth, but Mom was done—this was her limit.

Mom gave me the vanity, and I was so happy—for a moment. Then she told us that in the morning we were flying back to grandma and grandpas in Flushing Queens, leaving Dad behind. I was crushed, and although my sister was a toddler, she began to cry, as did my parents. Dad pleaded with Mom not to go, but she couldn't be dissuaded. The next day we packed up what we could carry, told Dad to find a home for our dog, and the vanity was left behind, never to be played with. I learned to never want something so badly and also learned to yearn for everything.

We flew back to Flushing to stay with my grandparents for a while until we could stabilize and find our next place to live. We left Dad behind, and I recall him waving and sobbing and pleading for us to remain as the plane took off from the runway and Dad became smaller and smaller. Another kaleidoscopic moment bringing into view another new beginning and leaving behind the shapes and forms of the past.

Dad eventually found a way back to my grandparents to reunite with us, and Mom accepted him back for yet one more chance. Grandma was so glad to see us all again and to meet my little sister. She was really glad to see Dad and shed tears of relief when he returned. Dad found a job in Ossining, New York, so we moved there next. The moving had become tiresome. I was eight years old and craved stability and security.

I asked Mom lots of questions, and I remember being told that I talked too much and asked too many questions. I had become quite precocious and relentless as well. I was so glad to be back in the warmth and safety of my grandparents, and especially being with my grandma again. The apartment smelled like matzo-ball soup, brisket of beef, tzimmes, matzo, charoset, and all of the other Hanukah foods and smells. We arrived on the fourth night of Hanukah, so the Hanukah candles were aflame and Grandpa recited the prayers over wine.

It turned out that my aunt picked us up at the airport, and my cousin told me about all the "colored people" that had moved into the neighborhood. I didn't miss a beat and asked "what colors?" This was my initiation into white privileged racism.

We stayed for a much shorter time this stay, and then headed off to Connecticut. My dad found a job at Pratt and Whitney, a maker of jets and other planes, and since dad had served in the air force this seemed hopeful. We said our good-byes again, but this time we weren't too sad, as we were back in the East and could more easily visit family.

Clay takes form.
Friendships develop.
Disappointment again.

TOWN ROADS
GLASTONBURY
CONNECTICUT DEPARTMENT OF TRANSPORTATION

SCALE

REVISED TO DEC. 31, 1973
REVISED TO SEPT 4 1974

GLASTONBURY, CONNECTICUT

DAD WANTED TO move closer to his brother's family, and I attended first grade in Glastonbury. I loved the school, as it was in a field in the woods and was a one-room schoolhouse. We would take hikes in the woods, and learning was exciting, and I was surrounded by birdsong and nature. I made friends easily, as I was talkative and outgoing. We used to go to the riverbank and play with the river clay, which felt so smooth and gooshy between my fingers and toes.

In Connecticut we lived in a bi-level apartment complex with loads of other kids living there, and we'd play outdoors together all the time. That's where I remember first playing "doctor" and challenging one another to strip nude inside of an old refrigerator box we'd found. We each took turns, but a parent on the second floor looked down and caught us and told all of the other parents, and we got into lots of trouble.

One great memory was of when Mom, my sister, our three friends and their mom, and two dogs filled up a car and traveled to our friends' family's home in Maine. We slept in bunkbeds, went clamming in the mornings, and had a wonderful adventure. We left our dads behind, as they both worked at Pratt and Whitney and had met there, and it turned out that we lived in the same apartment complex. Our friendship with this family restored my faith in having friends, and that friendship was possible and we have remained connected throughout the years, especially with the help of Facebook.

Midway through the school year, my mother told me that we had to move, and this made me so sad and so angry. Mom said that Dad had lost his job at Pratt and Whitney and told us that we had to move to a place in Ossining, New York, where Dad had found work at a local prison, Sing Sing. This made me scared, as working in a big dark prison was frightening. I wasn't looking forward to moving to Ossining. This also meant that Dad would be gambling whatever money he had in order to try to win us some food money. It was about this time that Dad was attending Gamblers Anonymous meetings and Mom attended Gam-Anon meetings, but the gambling never stopped for very long. Dad asked my uncle for money to tide us over. My uncle gave generously to Dad, never expecting it to be reimbursed.

I begged my parents to stay, but again, Dad was searching for a job far away. I was only a little girl who had no say and was powerless over my life's challenges, as children mostly are. I missed my toys we had to leave behind in Connecticut, but Mom told me that they had found new homes, so I didn't miss them so much. When we left Connecticut, I felt really sad. I loved my school and my friends, and I loved the one-room schoolhouse and the nature walks in the woods. I had lots of friends even though I was only six or seven years old. These times were a lot of fun, and I always had lots of playmates and met some long-term friends there that we remained in touch with through the years. While writing this chapter I was able to locate a childhood best friend whom I hadn't spoken with for over forty-eight years! It felt like nothing had changed as we chuckled while reminiscing about our shared childhood. What a gift—to reconnect with the one friend who stayed in my life through my parents' divorce and had once been my best friend. She told me that, to this day, when asked to create a security password question and answer she inserts my name as her childhood best friend. This was another kaleidoscopic overlay and gift of reconnecting that was a pedestal for the kaleidoscope to rest on.

But upon recollection, we were to leave again and move anew. I wonder if my parents knew of my pain and disappointment and sense of loss. I was heartbroken and didn't want to leave, so I didn't. I stomped my right foot and clenched my fist around the magical rabbit's foot grandma had given me and created a life I wanted, not the one we were living. It was like part of me stayed and thrived, and part of me had to go along with the incessant leaving. It really was a form of dissociation for survival. Like a kaleidoscope splitting off and creating new designs, our lives were filled with images, colors, and symbols of new beginnings, new endings, new landscapes, new sights, and new smells. Always a bit different each time.

When this part of the kaleidoscope turned, I went and lived with my family in Connecticut who lived about an hour away, or at least I wanted to. They had an old farmhouse and a pond, and on a visit with my dad one time—years later, after my parents' divorce—I held Dad's hand and watched as a great blue heron took flight. Great Blue Herons have since been my spiritual bird.

I loved the smell of hay and manure in my uncle's barn and enjoyed feeding his horse hay and oats. I loved the old house that was built in 1702 and smelled of smoke and burning fireplaces. I went to Camp Astawamah when visiting there during the summertime. It was a sleepaway camp that I loved attending. This was where I learned to love the wilderness and the outdoors. We boated, prayed, sang, did crafts, played capture the flag, toasted marshmallows, and made s'mores. These were some of my best memories. My mom and aunt and uncle would visit me at camp, and I told them that I wanted to stay among the trees and wildlife forever.

I imagined that I lived with my uncle's family for several months, but, truthfully, I used my memories of summer vacations spent there to shape my imaginal escape from life on the road. I reconnected with my parents after my fantasy was up. At my aunt and uncle's, I enjoyed that every night we would all have dinner together and talk about the day's events. My uncle would take us for hikes in the woods, and we would watch him ride his horse. The family always had a dog that never had to leave and go to another home, like our dogs. My aunt gave me loads of attention and made delicious rhubarb pie. I loved my four boy cousins. We played a lot, and they were more like brothers to me. We ran freely over the plush earth padded with spongy mosses. My family had dogs that also ran freely, and one year we brought our dog Tiffy for a visit, and she crossed the road and got hit by a car but, thankfully, not badly—and she made a full recovery.

These were the best years of my life, and I never wanted them to end. I didn't go to school for a while because I didn't know how long I'd be able to remain in my fantasy. I loved the weekends when we would all pile into the car and go either to a nature preserve, a little farm-like zoo, or a Native American powwow with sage burning and drum beats pounding and dancers dancing the friendship dance.

I loved my family and still remain close, as we are kindred spirits. I've collected many gems from living with my family, so it was time to rejoin my traveling family, and I wondered if they knew I wasn't with them in my mind and was lost in my escape fantasies. I had been living a fantasy as we drove to the next place where we were going to live for a while. I was really in need of a transfusion of love and stability—and less chaos and arguing.

My mother recently said that the moving had been a lot of fun and an adventure for her and Dad, but I was able to say that it wasn't fun for a new girl at each school I attended and that making and losing friendships was painful, as was having to leave behind belongings and pets. I knew that I'd visit my aunt and uncle every summer, and as an adult I actually lived with them for two years while completing my college education. Knowing I would see them didn't make the leaving so bad.

Batmobiles speed away.
Magic surrounds me.
Sleighing fast downhill.

OSSINING, NEW YORK

WE MOVED TO Ossining to try again some-
where new, yet not too far away to start again—
as my parents had reunited and they seemed
affectionate toward each other, holding hands and
hugging on the couch while we watched evening television
shows like "I Love Lucy" and "My Mother the Car." I loved
Batman and Robin the most. On my birthday, there was a
knock on the door, and a card was slid under the door. When
I opened the card, it was from Batman and Robin, wishing me
a happy birthday. I was so excited when Dad told me run to
the window to see the Batmobile going down the road. I ran
to the window as fast as I could. Although I missed seeing the
Batmobile, I treasured the card signed by Batman and Robin
that wished me a happy eighth birthday. The next time we
moved, the card was left behind.

Our fifth-floor, high-rise apartment was on a steep hill.
During a wintry wonderland of a storm, my dad and I rode a
sled from the top of the hill to the bottom. It was exhilarating,
and there was so much joy doing this with Dad and having

him home. Mom was working, and so was Dad, and things seem to be improving.

I had a little boyfriend by the name of David who was in second or third grade, and I went to a daycare center after school while my parents worked until they'd pick up my sister and me afterwards. When it was time to leave again—because, of course, it was *always* time to leave again (I was used to it by now)—my parents actually took me over to David's house, having contacted his parents, and we all sat down and had cookies and punch together. I was actually able to say goodbye to David, and this was the first time I had ever had the opportunity to say goodbye to someone I was leaving behind. I will always remember this because, through the years, I have had many friends and lovers who I would just walk away from—or cling too tightly to. For me, attachments ran deep while I was in them, but I also could easily walk away to start anew, sometimes without saying goodbye.

Sing Sing prison was located within walking distance of our apartment building. Everybody knew about the type of prisoners who were in there, and it was considered a very dangerous place. Sometimes there would be escapees from the prison, and this was always a little bit scary for me.

I remember enjoying Halloween at our apartment building and getting tons of candy from our neighbors. The people in this building were friendly, but there were many residents, so I learned to choose safe people to talk to and knew to stay away from those who made me feel scared inside with that tingly feeling in my belly. This was a darker Kaleidoscope than I was used to.

I had a best friend named Sharon, the same name as my

sister, and she used to do cartwheels as we were walking up and down the road because she was a gymnast. I really liked her; she was my best friend at the time, and I dreaded the moment when my parents would say that we were moving again. That day came, and we had to move back to Mount Vernon.

My parents were working on separating from one another. Although they loved each other, my father's gambling always got in the way and put us at risk of homelessness. My dad had lost his job again, and my mom felt more comfortable returning to Mount Vernon because that was the one place where she had lived the longest since coming to the United States. I said goodbye to Ossining and brought a few of my toys, thinking I had brought the Batman card, but I hadn't, and that really upset me more than anything. We did have a little dog, and the dog did come with us to our new apartment in Mount Vernon. I'm really happy that we didn't have to leave her behind with some random stranger in the building.

I had liked my school in this town and I had had a lot of friends. I did talk a lot, though. On my report card, the teacher wrote that I talk too much and I ask too many questions. This about sums up who I was. I was very precocious and inquisitive because there were so many things that took place in my life that were out of my control, and I did have loads of questions. I was beginning to understand that, as a child, you don't really have control. I could fantasize and make up stories and make believe my life wasn't the way it was, but the bottom line was that I had to live the life that my parents laid out for me whether I liked it or not. We returned to Mount Vernon for my parents to try one last time together. Then maybe their marriage would finally end.

Mom got a job at Reader's Digest, and we found an apartment and moved again. I got to say goodbyes to my friends and the first boyfriend I'd met at school. It was again sad to leave but by now I'd expected to move again. I think I would have excelled at school if I hadn't had to keep switching schools.

Friendships begin in earnest.
Defiance danced wildly.
Crowded high-rises towered above.

MOUNT VERNON, NEW YORK (SECOND TIME)

WE MOVED THREE times in and around Mount Vernon, yet we remained within the same school district and never had to leave our friends, toys, pets, and belongings behind ever again.

The first of those three apartments was on the third floor of a three-family house. When we moved in, we thought that we were at peace and could begin to stabilize at last—except that our parents had once again reunited. They constantly separated and reunited—only for Dad to leave again. Our friends from Glastonbury moved to nearby Scarsdale, and we'd get together for play dates and dinner parties. I liked seeing those friends again.

Once, when Dad left for a long time, and I never thought he'd return again, he showed up at the dance studio of my dance lesson. I was in the front of the class and saw his kaleidoscopic reflection in the mirrors. I became all choked up and had feelings of gladness and also feelings of sadness. Once again, he returned later that night, only to begin arguing with Mom about money and his gambling. This time my mother put her foot down and said that she was filing for a divorce, which was unheard of in their generation. It turned out that my sister and I were the only students at our school from a divorced family—yet another stigma separating us from our peers to overcome. Following the confirmation of divorce, Dad took off for two years and married another woman and brought her and her children to California and stayed a while, then left her with her children. We didn't hear from him at all during this time, so I thought that he had died, as this was the only thing that made any sense to me to explain why he was away for so long.

I was attending sixth grade at Columbus Elementary School, and it was a time when girls were allowed to wear pantsuits, and it was no longer mandatory to wear dresses to school. One day I was called down to the principal's office, and as I walked into her office, there sat my dad. I began to sob as I told him that I thought he was dead. I was so glad to see him. I think that I equate death with abandonment fears. He had come by to see me and my sister. He wasn't coming home to reunite, because Mom had moved on and wouldn't be giving him any more chances. And he wasn't given the key to our apartment.

Boy—was I happy to see him again. But I remember his anger at times. Once, when we were driving the wrong way into the city, he angrily turned our car onto the island heading toward the bridge. The brakes shrieked and the car jostled to a halt. It was very scary. I recall a time when he broke my mom's finger when they were fighting and he forcefully grabbed her hand. This was when she said that she was done with the marriage. I also remember a Fourth of July at an amusement park when he verbally threatened a patron who cut him off in the parking lot. This was frightening and unpredictable. Apparently, he had inherited some of Grandpa's rage.

From this point in time following the divorce, he would take my sister and I on visitations, and we would take the train to New York City, where he'd take us to fancy restaurants if he'd won at gambling, but only to use toilets at fancy hotels when he had no money to buy us a meal. Then we would grab snacks from street vendors. He would bring us to fancy restaurants in Manhattan—Windows on the World, Trader Vic's, the Plaza Hotel, Sign of the Dove. I loved going out to eat with him because at home we lived on food-stamp groceries. There was a stigma attached to using the colorful stamps that alerted everyone to our poverty.

When my sister didn't come on visits, Dad would tell me adult things, and of his gambling and other escapades. This made me feel uncomfortable but also that I was his favorite child, as he trusted me with his secrets. I felt like I was his girl-friend—without all of the kissing and stuff. He'd often give me money if he had it, and I'd feel guilty that my sister wasn't given any, so when I got home, I'd lie and tell her that Dad sent her money home with me, and I'd give her half of my money. It was all very confusing—and I wanted a dad without all of the lies and deceit and especially without having to hear of his gambling wins and losses.

I'm told that Dad got married a third time to a pretty lady in New Jersey. He got arrested for bouncing checks and spent several weeks in jail, to be bailed out by his wife and my uncle.

He eventually left her and jumped bail back into New York. I am also told that he became a devout Jewish man living amongst a group of Hasidim in Brooklyn. He changed his name to an alias and kept in touch with us on occasion, sometimes calling to beg for money when he was destitute. I hated to receive these calls because I couldn't help him, and it was heartbreaking. Eventually, I learned to tell him that I wouldn't bail him out. Up to then, I hadn't realized how sick he was.

The second Mount Vernon home was in a two-story house, where I had a great bedroom apart from my mom and sister, and I used to sneak in runaway friends to sleep there until morning, hiding them out and giving them shelter. There were lots of kids to play with, and we would play until dark. We'd play touch football and capture the flag. In the winter we'd find chunks of wax by the railroad tracks, and the older boys would make a bonfire, and we'd melt the wax and stick our hands into the molten wax, making creations. These are fun memories.

A memory that wasn't too much fun was when my mother's boyfriend stuck his tongue into my mouth. This was in broad daylight, when he dropped me off at a babysitting job. Before this, I had loved and trusted him. I told Mom, and even though she disbelieved my story, I was never allowed to be alone with him ever again. Until this happened, I was like his own daughter, and he would bring me to a family-run restaurant every Wednesday evening while Mom was working—and this was a weekly outing where I felt treasured.

During my adolescence I went with friends to numerous rock concerts and would often be so brazen that we'd sneak backstage to meet the rock stars. This was so much fun. I worked as a camp counselor in town and would also visit my aunt, uncle, and cousins every summer for a couple of weeks at a time.

We'd play outdoors, swim in the cold waters of the pond and enjoy home-cooked meals each night. I remember twice sliding down the wooden stairs in the old part of the house, and the story goes that I never stopped talking as I bounced down the steps, and everyone showed concern but were also chuckling.

I remember washing my hair outside during a torrential storm, and I can recall the millions of stars in the night sky. We all used to play ping-pong, which was lots of fun. This was my favorite place to be. When I got older, I did in fact live with this family for two years as I attended a local university.

Our third and last move was to a five-story apartment building with an elevator, laundry room, and ornate lobby with a fireplace and artwork. I could smell the mixed odors of foods made by the tenants of the building, and they were welcoming and reminded me of my grandparents' apartment building. We had incinerators for our garbage, which I found to be fascinating.

It was this residence where I was to meet my first husband and also a best friend of mine. They lived on the fifth floor, and we lived on the first floor. My adolescence is a whole other story, as this was the 1970s—and we experimented with sex, drugs, and rock and roll for real! Fun times—yet crazy times too. Too crazy for our underdeveloped selves.

Mom got remarried to a stable, disciplined man, and we all breathed a sigh of relief to be home at last, at least initially. Home means an enjoyable, happy place where you can live, laugh, and learn. It's a place where you are loved, respected, and cared for. But when you look at it from the outside, home is just a house. Our home wasn't peaceful or loving when my defiance flared up and I would constantly argue with my step-father, and at times the arguments became almost violent. I also fought a lot for my mother's attention, and I didn't like to witness her becoming submissive to her husband. I needed help to release my built-up anger, but no one sought help for me. I was the spokesman for our family, and my sister was the good child. So I became the bad, outspoken one.

We had finally landed and were no longer on the run, but I still wasn't at home within myself and wondered if I'd ever be.

I have always had a recurring dream of driving on winding roads endlessly searching for a place that I could truly call *home*. Years later, I finally found that place within myself, and I no longer have to keep searching. It has taken me a lifetime to find it—and now, at age sixty, I have finally settled into my forever home, and wild horses couldn't drag me away. I have love, beauty, stability, and a firm foundation to keep me rooted. I never knew that home could feel this good. We live near the river and enjoy all sorts of wildlife year-round—especially my beloved herons three months of the year. Coincidentally, I have developed symptoms of agoraphobia, which makes leav-ing home especially difficult. The irony of this is not lost on me.

A Heron landing in murky waters,
keenly observing her surroundings,
flying home to nest in the trees.

EPILOGUE

The illusion of a kaleidoscope can be witnessed in my refrigerator as foods move around the refrigerator making spaces, patterns, and formations. An empty refrigerator generates empty spaces and hunger and longing, so I bought a smaller refrigerator that always appears bountiful and filled to the brim.

My husband Gary is my home and my strength and has provided strong love, compassion, play, joy, and acceptance. He has taught me what security and stability feel like. We live in an earthy smelling home, partially because of the lighting of incense, sage, and Palo Alto. This house has no bad aromas, no mustiness or staleness, and was a good home from the time we first settled in. Here, along the Hudson River in Upstate New York, there are herons and eagles and much other wildlife surrounding us. I no longer have any wish to move elsewhere, which as an adult often troubled me as a sort of repetition compulsion.

Writing this book became like a kaleidoscope; as I gained new memories, my story constantly took on a different hue and recreated itself. Sometimes this was frustrating, as I wished to tell a linear tale, but I could not help that the book took me on twists and turns I didn't even know existed. But as I wrote, I learned that the gifts I gathered on the road and in numerous abodes created my life's kaleidoscope, filling me with wonder and strength for the challenges that would come later.

I couldn't have told my story without Gary. He began the journey of this telling lying alongside me on the rug beneath the "World's Largest Kaleidoscope" and has encouraged me all along the way. I later found out that Gary had also moved several times, and his parents were divorced as well, and he lived with his grandmother and aunt periodically. Perhaps my story is partially his story too.

One challenge I should have seen coming was my struggle with agoraphobia following a medical procedure in 2018. I just couldn't leave home, no matter what. I missed weddings, my children's life celebrations, funerals, and life in general. I still struggle with these symptoms to a lesser degree. But, as you can deduce, I love my home and being at home, and maybe this is the long sigh following my life on the road of trying on homes that never fit. Homes too small, too smelly, too large, and not cozy enough. This home was made for me, and I'm not looking to move again. And now we have the joy of my daughter, grandson, and son-in-law living with us during the Pandemic.

My kaleidoscopic journey is complete, and all of the brilliant, fragmented shards have been rearranged into a radiant new whole. For now, this is where my story ends. Thank you for bearing witness to my telling of my life story up until age nine.

GRATITUDE

To MY DEAR book coach, Cait Johnson, who gently yet determinedly encouraged my story be told in its complexity. My parents, for giving me a life of wonder and surprise and joie de vivre and an understanding of being prepared to let go of all that mattered. My mom, for helping with the timeline of my telling. My younger sister, for always being there for me even when we saw life differently. My children, their spouses and partners, and my two amazing grandsons. My friend Debbie, whom I recently spoke with after forty-eight years(!) —for reminding me that as a child I did have a friend. My Aunt Irene and my Uncle Morty, for providing me with solid memories of Connecticut and Oklahoma.

The World's Largest Kaleidoscope Catskills Museum, for initiating this story.

My spouse Gary, for encouraging my memoir and listening to the revisions over and over. For loving me through painful memories—and forever my muse, my clown—making me laugh and cry tears of joy.

My devoted companion dog, Maizy.

My Creator—the Great Spirit, God.